SONG BOOK

1

NAKED CITY
OF DARKNESS

Robert William Stephen

Print information available on the last page

Rev. date: 07/17/2015

To order additional copies of this book, contact:
Xlibris
1-800-455-039
www.xlibris.com.au
Orders@Xlibris.com.au

Song Book 1

Naked City of Darkness
Songs By Robert Stephen
Art By Christine Armstrong

Dedicated to Christine Armstrong

ACKNOWLEDGEMENTS

I would like to give thanks to the following:
Central Commercial Printer Bathurst
Leigh Berry for her beautiful hand writing
Jim Armstrong for his beautiful hand writing
My Mom for financial support

1) Poem Christine   Light

2) Seat   Light

3) In Black Room   Light

4) Goodnight Christine   Dark

5) Christine   Dark

6) She Slips into Darkness   Dark

7) Baby's Gone on me   Dark

8) There for Me   Light

9) To Be Alone   Mellow

10) Pale Deaths   Mellow

11) Girl is Magic   Light

12) The Mouse and the Cat   Light

13) Now She's Everything   Light

14) You Dropped Me   Light

15) It's the Sky When Day has Gone   Dark

16) Skin and Bone for the Devil   Dark

17) At Lizette's   Dark

18) The Naked Lies   Dark

19) If I Loved You   Light

20) Straight Line   Mellow

21) When I'm Driving Under Darkness   Light

22) King Nothing   Light

23) Comfort in the Treasures of Love   Light

24) And So It's Over She Said   Light

25) With a Pickup Line   Light

26) Cells are Divided   Light

27) My Delight   Light

28) It's Sweet Thing   Light

29) The Scattered Pieces of You and Me   Mellow

30) Into the Flow Under Darkness   Dark

31) Son of the Devil   Dark

32) Hollow and the Emptiness   Dark

33) On the Needle Tonight   Dark

34) Father Browns Heroin   Dark

35. ???   Light

36) The Last Goodbye   Dark

37) Outside the palace   Light

Light 19

Mellow 4

Dark 14

YOUR NAME WAS CHRISTINE

Your Name was Christine
Your Body was Pristine
Your House was Clean
You were Never Mean
Your Love was Obscene
Your Heart of Gold Gleamed
Like the Mirror you had Seen
And behind it was Clean
You were Like a Love Machine
Your Love Beamed
For All to see All Humanity
You were the Woman the Woman for me
And will Always be

"SEAT"

A Naked Woman is a seat
for me
While I play my Guitar
She drew me and her
And she was Naked
I was playing my Guitar
She was Naked
She was right there under my ASS

While I played my Guitar
She was Naked
She was there
She was a seat
A Beautiful Woman
Was a Seat
A Naked Woman
Was a Seat

MICHELS MILK

Sept 2014

Michels Milk
Michels Cream
My Sleep
Michels Dream
My Dream
Michels Milk
Popstar
In the Charts
At No One
Where it Starts
Where it Starts
Where it Starts
Michels Milk

SIT AND WATCH TV

In a black room
With a hanging light
In a black room
Nothing on TV
Nothing Special to me
Nothing grabs me
On TV that I see
Just TV and me
In a black room
In a black room
In a black room

GOODNIGHT CHRISTINE

27/8/14.

Say goodbye my angel
Say goodbye and sweet dreams
Say goodbye my angel
Say goodnight my sweet Christine

I will always love you
With a love that burns so true
I will always have a love that burns for you

Say goodbye my angel
Say goodnight and sweet dreams
Say goodbye my angel
Say goodnight my sweet Christine

It's time to say goodbye
I can tell from the look in your eyes
Soon you'll leave my side
It's time to say goodnight

Say goodbye my angel
Say goodnight and sweet dreams
Say goodbye my angel
Say goodnight my sweet Christine
Say goodbye its goodbye Christine

Say goodbye and goodnight Christine
Say goodbye
Say goodbye now honey
Say goodbye
And goodnight my Christine.

CHRISTINE

1/9/14.

I used to rely on you
To do the things I need to do
And now the hardest part
Is making a start
All fresh and new
Cause Im weak cause Im weak Cause Im weak
I became used to you
I always loved seeing you
Now I am so blue
I just can't leave you.
I need something to see me though
Cause Im weak Cause Im weak Cause Im weak
I was only strong when I was with you
You made me able to do
I will always need you
With courage and love
I will get through
I will never forget you
Christine Christine Christine Christine
Christine Christine Christine Christine

SHE SLIPS INTO DARKNESS

About 3am
Never to be seen
Never seen again
I lost my Girlfriend
On whom I depend
I not only lost her
but my bestfriend
It's the end Christine
It's the end for you and me

She slips into darkness
About 3am
And I was her witness
I was there til the end

THERE FOR ME

27 August 2014

Baby got brown eyes
Baby got brown hair
Baby never lies
She's always there
And I care And I care And I care
For her
And I care And I care Yes I care
For baby
Baby got a nice face
Baby got a nice shape
And she watches her weight
And what can I say
And She's there And She's there And She's there
For me
And she's there And she's there Yes she's there
For baby
I love my baby
Baby loves me too.

BABY'S GONE ON ME

27/8/14.

My Baby she died on me
My Baby she had to leave
That Baby meant everything to me
Yeah you know she was so sweet
She was special
So special to me
And now I'm so lonely
Yeah so Fucking lonely
It's all up to me
It's my time to greive
She was special
So special to me
So special
So special to me.

TO BE ALONE

24/8/14

When the fire's high
And the water's low
There is nowhere else
I'd rather go
If you want to see
The fires glow
Get up real close
And see the show
As the fire burns
You will know
What it is
To be alone.

PALE DEATHS 1992.

Another pale death
Another white man with Indian blood on his hand
Another killer winter
And the Slaughter begins
With another pale death
Another pale death
Yet another pale death
Another pale death
Another white man with Indian blood on his hands
Another killer Winter
An Indian tragedy
Another pale death
Yet another pale death
Pale then blue
Pale then gone
Pale deaths.

GIRL IS MAGIC

If something different
Is what you seek
Could take a month, a year
Or even a week
From strength to strength
Forget the meek
From length to length
The distance that we keep
The girl is magic
What can I say
Her life is tragic
And fading away
She'd like to stab it
The poison vein
She'd like to have it
Just the same.

THE MOUSE AND THE CAT

Slow and fast
Nice catch
Dirty rat
Nice and fat
Nice and fat
The mouse and the cat
The dirty rat
He stole the catch
Sit down
Pass it around
Go to ground
Make a sound
Play at the pound
Only to confound
Play it around.

NOW SHE'S EVERYTHING

20 November 2013

Now she's free and now she's clean
And now she's someone else
Now she's him and now she's me
And now she's on drugs
Now she's seen and now she's heard
What is the final word
Now she's mean and I say
What a girl.
Now she's free
Now she's not
Now she's clean
Now she's hot
Now she speaks
And she's off.

YOU DROPPED ME

I said sorry but I can't help myself
You said sorry put me back on the shelf
So now I hurry chasing after you
But you avoid me and do what you do.
You do it so well I can't even tell
You take and drop me straight into hell
You dropped me
You dropped me yeah yeah yeah.

IT'S THE SKY WHEN DAY HAS GONE

One day it's gonna fall
One day will kill us all
One day Death makes his call
Then one day will be no more.
And then the night it's gonna fall
It's the sky when day has gone
When the day has gone

We bring it in by the darkness
Then it lives under night
And it preys on the weak ones
It steals their sight

Then one day forever more
We find the sun has gone
And the world is cold
And we're at war
And then the night is gonna fall
It's the sky when day has gone
When the day has gone.

And then the daylight becomes another lie
It just gets darker the harder we try
Searching the darkness for some light
When the night has struck us blind
It's the sky it's gonna fall
It's the sky when day has gone
When the day has gone

It's gonna fall on us all
On a day when the day has gone
On a day when the light is lost
And we'll scream up at the darkness
It's the sky it's gonna fall
It's the sky when the day has gone

When the day has gone.

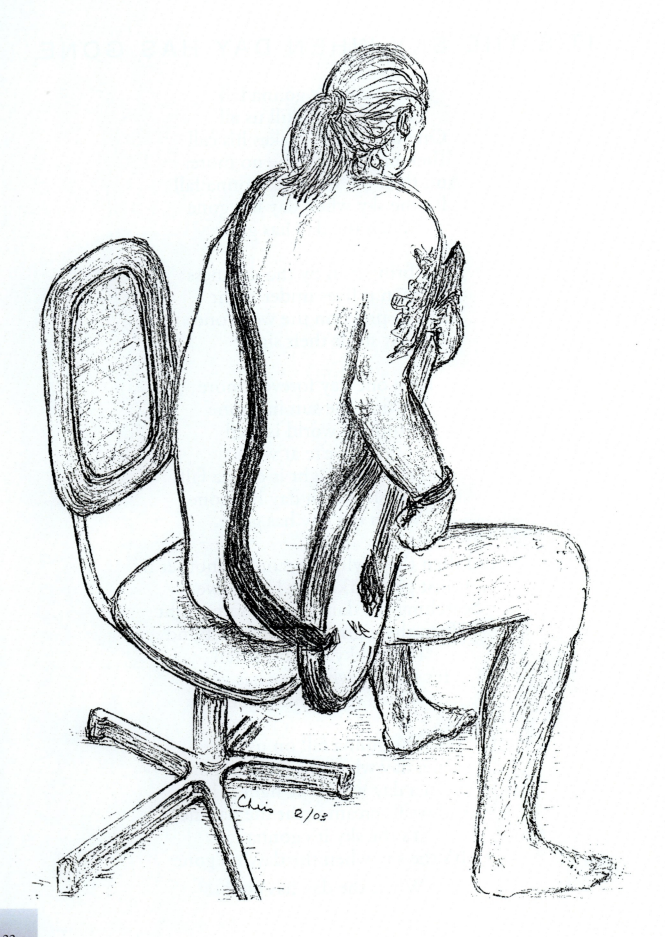

Chris 2/03

SKIN AND BONE FOR THE DEVIL

Money, lust, and greed
Money, lust, and greed, oh greed
Ooh wah ooh, you know it's true
Ooh wah ooh, when it's got you, yeah
Money lust and greed, yeah
Money lust and greed ah ah
Money lust and greed oww
Money lust and greed, it's the devil's dream.
As I see them send their pounds of flesh to him
Skin and bone for the devil
Gone, gone to the devil
Through the fires of passion
Straight to the fires of hell
To the devil and the beast thing
Oh for the death of innocence
He says I must collect all debts
'Cause nothing is free
My God, help me
I'm just skin and bone
Skin and bone
Oh for the devil
Oh for the devil no
But skin and bone I am
Like a skeleton I am for him.
For no greater evil
Then the weight of my vices
'Cause nothing is free
God help me
I'm just skin and bone
Skin and bone
Oh for the devil
Oh for the devil no
My beautiful soul has gone
My beautiful soul has gone
To the devil.

AT LIZETTE'S

She throws he chain as fire on a gold ring
Into the air we will both breathe
Into my deepest desire
And the heat is rising up tonight
But that's alright
It's what I like it's just a
This kind of heat burns so damn hot
It burns a hole straight through my soul
Into its core
Makes me forget now
What I came in for
Inside her love
I let her darkness into my soul
And then her darkness left my soul
Barren
And corrupt as I let myself go
Man I'm really gone
It's been so long now that I think it's evil
But I know that it's special
Makes my delusions real
It feeds my passion
I know that it's poison
It's the fusion of the flow in my mind
In my mind
Yeah yeah
Yeah yeah
At Lizette's
Yeah at Lizette's

THE NAKED LIES

How can we find him
Another place to hide
A place to lie
A place to cry about yesterday's lies
He once believed in
But he won't be stung twice
He won't believe again

The naked lies
He once believed in
The naked lies
From his angel's sweet lips
The naked lies come
And everything is lost
'Cause the naked lies
Are the stingers

How can we find him
Just a little fun
To help him think
To forget someone
Is never easily done
And it's never any fun

'Cause the naked lies
Cause so much pain
And the naked lies
Sting again and again

And the naked lies
Stung once, stung twice
The naked lies
Are the stingers

The naked lies
She said she loved him
He looked into her eyes
But something tells him here they
come again.

IF I LOVED YOU

If I loved you
I would care for you
I would feel for you
I'd feel blue without you
I could never want to hurt you

But I would give to you
Oh everything that I could
Cause in my heart I'd know it's true
And all my body and my love
Would be all for you
I could never give you up
Cause if I loved you
You'd be my addiction

But with the sweetest of hearts
You'd be the only girl I'd want
Ever since your smile stole my heart
And your deep blue eyes and soft warm touch
I could never give you up
Cause if I loved you
You'd be my addiction

STRAIGHT LINE

Straight line, straight line
The way you lay so fine
When life's insane and blind
And so are you, so am I
Well you set me up to be crucified
I'm running out of time
Cos you set me up to be crucified
And I'm running out of time
Straight line
Straight line
For better this better that, they say
When you only get the chances you get I say
Some luck is good, some luck is bad
One heart gets battered one gets bashed
And there is no difference
Can be defined
Straight line, straight line
The straight line, the straight line
The straight line, the straight line
That lays so fine, that lays so fine
The straight line, the straight line
Straight line.

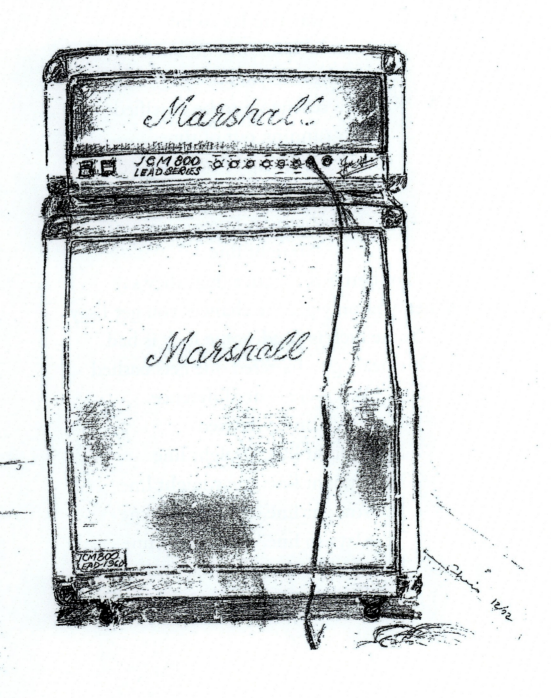

KING NOTHING

Yeah I've always been nothing
And that's easy to see
But it makes me feel something
And that's all that I need
All that I need.

But at least I'm honest
And I keep my lyrics clean
And they make it not so hard
For me to believe that

Chorus
I can do anything
When it's in me
And it might just be an empty dream
But I'm the hollow King Nothing
Yeah the king of nothing
King Nothing

Without lyrics I'm just empty
But I'm as guilty as sin
Cos I do it cos I like it
I can be nothing's king
Oh then

Chorus

COMFORT IN THE TREASURES OF LOVE

You can find comfort in the treasures of her love
You can find your pleasure in the treasures of her love
Repeat

But don't forget to love her
Even if she's not nice

Then she'll set your soul on fire burning through the night.
And you can find her in the house of lost souls, you know where to find

Repeat

But if you find out her heart isn't gold
But if you find out her heart isn't gold

Then it's cold, cold and your love is lost
Your intentions were wasted on another lost cause.

Repeat

AND SO IT'S OVER SHE SAID

You know it's over she said to me
As she was packing to leave
Said it wasn't you baby, it wasn't me
It was your insane jealousy
Oh but you didn't
Listen to me

So now she's gone far away from me
All the way to Junee
When will she be back my God
Will she ever return to me

Another winter is over
But I'm still cold and alone
My broken heart must have frozen
Frozen she said my true love
Then
I'm just your friend now she said
I'm just your friend she said.
And so it's over
And so it's over she said

You know it's over baby yeah
Your jealousy
You know it's over baby yeah
She said to me.

16 JANUARY 2014

WITH A PICKUP LINE

My favourite kind of story line
Is where a guy meets a girl
With a pickup line
He sees the sweetness in her eyes
He puts his hand on her thigh
Then says "come on babe,
Come home with me tonight
And I'll make you feel OK
It'll be alright"
With a pickup line, yeah
With a pickup line
With a pickup line, yeah
Or to be there at the same time
See this guy meet this girl
Maybe hear his line
Take it for myself
And see if it works as my line
I'll say "come on babe,
Come home with me tonight
And I'll make you feel OK
It'll be alright.
With a pickup line, yeah
With a pickup line
With a pickup line, yeah
That works every time yeah.

ROB'S SONGS

8 October 2013

CELLS ARE DIVIDED

Cells are divided
I walk across the wire
My feet are sore and tired
My eyes are open wide
She invites me inside
When I'm inside her
I'm so excited
My cells are divided
My cells are divided yeah.

MY DELIGHT

I'm gonna try
Close my eyes I can fly
I don't ask why
Just a shy proof of life
Man and wife more strife
Lost light my fight
My wife black night
White light second sight
My delight my delight

IT'S SWEET THING

Mmmmmmm
I wish I was closer
To that peach soft skin
Can't tell right away what colour her hair is yet
Have to wait till she hits the light again
Hope she's a sweet thing
Yeah she's a sweet thing
It's my sweet thing
It's sweet thing

15 JANUARY 2014

THE SCATTERED PIECES OF YOU AND ME

You're mine forever, baby
With your eyes so blue.
You're mine forever now angel
Eyes turn blue
But I won't leave you, leave you
I could never leave you
When served up to me from foreign places
Return memories and I can't sleep
Served up to me in torn up pictures
Of you and me
Now my scarred memories
Of the scattered pieces
From losing you to my enemies
And the scattered pieces
From you over me
At night
Especially
I won't forget you
I won't forget you
I won't forget you
You know who-oo-oo-oo-oo.

INTO THE FLOW UNDER DARKNESS

Gonna came out from under this blanket of madness
That stifled my light for too long.
And I'm gonna write a story all about it
Cos I want to tell everyone

About the darkness
That's living under darkness
Under darkness overnight
And into the flow now

And I'm gonna write about all of the sadness
That's eaten into my heart
Yeah I'll tell you about my time under darkness
And the nights when tears flowed
Into the madness
With her black kiss
Under darkness overnight

It's been living there
On the other side
It's been hidden
Under darkness overnight
And I've known this all my life
But I'm in with the flow now
I'm under darkness overnight.

SON OF THE DEVIL

It's a dangerous game
Why do we play
Put any two hearts back to back
One could be white, and one black
We just say Son of the Devil's in love
With an angel
We see them lying together in lust
On a halo
But his nature is of pain
She's just an innocent angel
It would hurt him to care for her
So he will break her heart
Then say
It's a dangerous game
When angels and devils play
And every heart breaks
When it ends these days
She was a
Son of the Devil's Angel
She was.

HOLLOW AND THE EMPTINESS

Pardon me thou bleeding piece of earth
For I am meek and humble with these butchers
My hunger is a cold burning desire
Just a small flame burning in my vein
Turned into a flameless fire
That was cold as ice
I don't want your water now
I want your advice
On all those little things that I forgot
About being me when you're gone
I wind an endless circle around the rim of my glass
I see the hunger returns to you, it's home at last
At home in your darkness feeding off your past
But it's a shallow grave, your cover never lasts
And if evil is the darkness
Then you are the night
Alright.
And you're so cold
That you deserve
Whatever you get from this world
With all the payback you've earned
Domme adara de dracules
My God, save me from the vampires.

ON THE NEEDLE TONIGHT

Looks like another long drive
I've seen all of the signs
It's always the same ones
I'm up all night
Until daylight
No I don't mind I don't mind
It's just my vice
On the Needle Tonight
When my fingers touch
that white shit
On the Needle Tonight
And I Know the needle is no friend
I know it's my worse enemy in fact
But I want feelings all the time
that I can't get but it can give
the Needle shoots it in for me
And I know I'll die
well before I suceed
or become an oldman
And all the money I've spent
Over & over again
Will never be enough
To buy my life back again
On the Needle Tonight.

FATHER BROWNS HEROIN

10th Sept 2014

Father Brown went to town
Coming down from Heroin
Riding on al cloud looking down
Off the ground on Heroin

THE LAST GOODBYE

This time's
Our last goodbye
I've fixed my wings
Now I'm gonna fly
Sleep, you'll sleep tonight
As I fly out of your light
The last goodbye
Cos our love, our love has died
Inside our hearts, inside our minds
There's no more tears left
We have to cry
No more flowers bought
Just to die
The last goodbye
The last goodbye
So long, goodnight God bless and all that.

Robbie J. Hendrix